EXAMINATION OF THE PROPHECIES

THOMAS PAINE

EXAMINATION OF THE PROPHECIES

Thomas Paine

IAP © 2009

IAP. Printed in Scotts Valley, CA - USA.

Paine, Thomas.

Examination of the Prophecies / Thomas Paine – 1st ed.

1. Religion.   2. Prophecies.

TABLE OF CONTENTS

INTRODUCTION

The passages called Prophecies of, or concerning, Jesus Christ, in the Old Testament may be classed under the two following heads.

First, those referred to in the four books of the New Testament, called the four Evangelists, Matthew, Mark, Luke, and John.

Secondly, those which translators and commentators have, of their own imagination, erected into prophecies, and dubbed with that title at the head of the several chapters of the Old Testament. Of these it is scarcely worth while to waste time, ink, and paper upon; I shall, therefore, confine myself chiefly to those referred to in the aforesaid four books of the New Testament. If I show that these are not prophecies of the person called Jesus Christ, nor have reference to any such person, it will be perfectly needless to combat those which translators or the church have invented, and for which they had no other authority than their own imagination.

I begin with the book called the Gospel according to St. Matthew.

THE BOOK OF MATTHEW

In i. 18, it is said, "Now the birth of Jesus Christ was on this wise: When his mother Mary was espoused to Joseph, before they came together, SHE WAS FOUND WITH CHILD OF THE HOLY GHOST." -- This is going a little too fast; because to make this verse agree with the next it should have said no more than that she was found with child; for the next verse says, "Then Joseph her husband, being a just man, and not willing to make her a public example, was minded to put her away privately." Consequently Joseph had found out no more than that she was with child, and he knew it was not by himself.

Ver. 20, 21. "And while he thought of these things, [that is whether he should put her away privately, or make a public example of her,] behold the Angel of the Lord appeared to him IN A DREAM [that is, Joseph dreamed that an angel appeared unto him] saying, Joseph, thou son of David, fear not to take unto thee Mary thy wife, for that which is conceived in her is of the Holy Ghost. And she shall bring forth a son, and call his name Jesus; for he shall save his people from their sins."

Now, without entering into any discussion upon the merits or demerits of the account here given, it is proper to observe, that it has no higher authority than that of a dream; for it is impossible to a man to behold any thing in a dream but that which he dreams of. I ask not, therefore, whether Joseph if there was such a man had such a dream or not, because admitting he had, it proves nothing. So wonderful and irrational is the faculty of the mind in dream, that it acts the part of all the characters its imagination creates, and what it thinks it hears from any of them is no other than what the roving rapidity of its own imagination invents. It is therefore nothing to me what Joseph dreamed of; whether of the fidelity or infidelity of his wife. I pay no regard to my own dreams, and I should be weak indeed to put faith in the dreams of another.

The verses that follow those I have quoted, are the words of the writer of the book of Matthew. "Now, [says he,] all this [that is, all this dreaming and this pregnancy] was done that it might be fulfilled which was spoken of the Lord by the Prophet, saying, Behold a virgin shall be with child, and shall bring forth a son, and they shall call his name Emmanuel, which being interpreted, is, God with us.

This passage is in Isaiah vii. 14, and the writer of the book of Matthew endeavors to make his readers believe that this passage is a prophecy of the person called Jesus Christ. It is no such thing, and I go to show it is not. But it is first necessary that I explain the occasion of these words being spoken by Isaiah. The reader will then easily perceive that so far from their being a prophecy of Jesus Christ, they have not the least reference to such a person, nor to any thing that could happen in the time that Christ is said to have lived, which was about seven hundred years after the time of Isaiah. The case is this;

On the death of Solomon the Jewish nation split into two monarchies: one called the kingdom of Judah, the capital of which was Jerusalem: the other the kingdom of Israel, the capital of which was Samaria. The kingdom of Judah followed the line of David, and the kingdom of Israel that of Saul; and these two rival monarchies frequently carried on fierce wars against each other.

At the time Ahaz was king of Judah, which was in the time of Isaiah, Pekah was king of Israel; and Pekah joined himself to Rezin, king of Syria, to make war against Ahaz, king of Judah; and these two kings marched a confederated and powerful army against Jerusalem. Ahaz and his people became alarmed at their danger, and "their hearts were moved as the trees of the wood are moved with the wind." Isaiah vii. 3.

In this perilous situation of things, Isaiah addresses himself to Ahaz, and assures him in the name of the Lord, (the cant phrase of all the prophets,) that these two kings should not succeed against him; and to assure him that this should be the case, (the case was however directly contrary,[1]) tells Ahaz to ask a sign of the Lord. This Ahaz declined doing, giving as a reason, that he would not tempt the Lord; upon which Isaiah, who pretends to be sent from God, says, ver. 14, "Therefore the Lord himself shall give you a sign, behold a virgin shall conceive and bear a son -- Butter and honey shall he eat, that he may know to refuse the evil and chose the good -- For before the child shall know to refuse the evil and chose the good, the land which thou abhorrest shall be forsaken of both her kings" -- meaning the king of Israel and the king of Syria who were marching against him.

Here then is the sign, which was to be the birth of a child, and that child a son; and here also is the time limited for the accomplishment of the sign, namely, before the child should know to refuse the evil and chose the good.

---

[1] II. Chron. xxviii. I. Ahaz was twenty years old when he began to reign. and he reigned sixteen years in Jerusalem, but he did not that which was right in the sight of the Lord. -- ver. 5. Wherefore the Lord his God delivered him into the hand of the king of Syria, and they smote him, and carried away a great multitude of them captive and brought them to Damascus; and he was also delivered into the hand of the king, of Israel, who smote him with a great slaughter. Ver. 6. And Pekah (king of Israel) slew in Judah an hundred and twenty thousand in one day. -- ver. 8. And the children of Israel carried away captive of their brethren two hundred thousand women, sons, and daughters.

The thing, therefore, to be a sign of success to Ahaz, must be something that would take place before the event of the battle then pending between him and the two kings could be known. A thing to be a sign must precede the thing signified. The sign of rain must be before the rain.

It would have been mockery and insulting nonsense for Isaiah to have assured Ahaz as a sign that these two kings should not prevail against him, that a child should be born seven hundred years after he was dead, and that before the child so born should know to refuse the evil and choose the good, he, Ahaz, should be delivered from the danger he was then immediately threatened with.

But the case is, that the child of which Isaiah speaks was his own child, with which his wife or his mistress was then pregnant; for he says in the next chapter, (Is. viii. 2), "And I took unto me faithful witnesses to record, Uriah the Priest, and Zechariah the son of Jeberechiah; and I went unto the Prophetess, and she conceived and bear a son and he says, at ver. 18 of the same chapter, "Behold I and the children whom the Lord hath given me are for signs and for wonders in Israel."

It may not be improper here to observe, that the word translated a virgin in Isaiah, does not signify a virgin in Hebrew, but merely a 'young woman.' The tense is also falsified in the translation. Levi gives the Hebrew text of Isaiah vii. 14, and the translation in English with it -- "Behold a young woman is with child and beareth a son;"[2] The expression, says he, is in the present tense. This translation agrees with the other circumstances related of the birth of this child which was to be a sign to Ahaz. But as the true translation could not have been imposed upon the world as a prophecy of a child to be born seven hundred years afterwards, the Christian translators have falsified the original: and instead of making Isaiah to say, behold a young woman is with child and beareth a son, they have made him to say, "Behold a virgin shall conceive and bear a son. It is, however, only necessary for a person to read Isaiah vii. and viii., and he will be convinced that the passage in question is no prophecy of the person called Jesus Christ. I pass on to the second passage quoted from the Old Testament by the New, as a prophecy of Jesus Christ.

Matthew ii. 1-6. "Now when Jesus was born in Bethlehem of Judea, in the days of Herod the king, behold there came wise men from the East to Jerusalem, saying, where is he that is born king of the Jews? For we have seen his star in the East, and are come to worship Him. When Herod the king heard these things he was troubled, and all Jerusalem with him; and when he had gathered all the chief priests and scribes of the people together, he demanded of them where Christ should be born. And they said

---

[2] A Defence of the Old Testament." By David Levi. London, 1797. -- Editor.

14

unto him, In Bethlehem, in the land of Judea: for thus it is written by the prophet, And thou Bethlehem, in the land of Judea, ant not the least among the Princes of Judah, for out of thee shall come a Governor that shall rule my people Israel." This passage is in Micah v. 2.

I pass over the absurdity of seeing and following a star in the day time, as a man would a 'Will with the whip,' or a candle and lantern at night; and also that of seeing it in the east, when themselves came from the east; for could such a thing be seen at all to serve them for a guide, it must be in the west to them. I confine myself solely to the passage called a prophecy of Jesus Christ.

The book of Micah, in the passage above quoted, v. 2, is speaking of some person, without mentioning his name, from whom some great achievements were expected; but the description he gives of this person, ver. 5, 6, proves evidently that it is not Jesus Christ, for he says, "and this man shall be the peace, when the Assyrian shall come into our land: and when he shall tread in our palaces, then shall we raise up against him [that is, against the Assyrian] seven shepherds and eight principal men. And they shall waste the land of Assyria with the sword, and the land of Nimrod on the entrance thereof; thus shall He [the person spoken of at the head of the second verse] deliver us from the Assyrian, when he cometh into our land, and when be treadeth within our borders."

This is so evidently descriptive of a military chief, that it cannot be applied to Christ without outraging the character they pretend to give us of him. Besides which, the circumstances of the times here spoken of, and those of the times in which Christ is said to have lived, are in contradiction to each other. It was the Romans, and not the Assyrians that had conquered and were in the land of Judea, and trod in their palaces when Christ was born, and when he died, and so far from his driving them out, it was they who signed the warrant for his execution, and he suffered under it.

Having thus shown that this is no prophecy of Jesus Christ, I pass on to the third passage quoted from the Old Testament by the New, as a prophecy of him. This, like the first I have spoken of, is introduced by a dream. Joseph dreameth another dream, and dreameth that he seeth another angel. The account begins at Matthew ii. 13. "The angel of the Lord appeared to Joseph in a dream, saying, Arise and take the young child and his mother and flee into Egypt, and be thou there until I bring thee word: For Herod will seek the life of the young child to destroy him. When he arose he took the young child and his mother by night and departed into Egypt: and was there until the death of Herod, that it might be fulfilled which was spoken of the Lord by the prophet, saying, Out of Egypt have I called my son."

This passage is in the book of Hosea, xi. I. The words are, "When Israel was a child then I loved him and called my son out of

Egypt. As they called them so they went from them, they sacrificed unto Baalim and burnt incense to graven images."

This passage, falsely called a prophecy of Christ, refers to the children of Israel coming out of Egypt in the time of Pharaoh, and to the idolatry they committed afterwards. To make it apply to Jesus Christ, he then must be the person who sacrificed unto Baalim and burnt incense to graven images; for the person called out of Egypt by the collective name, Israel, and the persons committing this idolatry, are the same persons, or the descendants of them. This then can be no prophecy of Jesus Christ, unless they are willing to make an idolator of him. I pass on to the fourth passage called a prophecy by the writer of the book of Matthew.

This is introduced by a story told by nobody but himself, and scarcely believed by any body, of the slaughter of all the children under two years old, by the command of Herod. A thing which it is not probable should be done by Herod, as he only held an office under the Roman government, to which appeals could always be had, as we see in the case of Paul. Matthew, however, having made or told his story, says, ii. 17, 18, "Then was fulfilled that which was spoken by Jeremy the prophet, saying, -- 'In Ramah was there a voice heard, lamentation, and weeping and great mourning, Rachel weeping for her children, and would not be comforted because they were not."

This passage is in Jeremiah xxxi. 15; and this verse, when separated from the verses before and after it, and which explain its application, might with equal propriety be applied to every case of wars, sieges, and other violence, such as the Christians themselves have often done to the Jews, where mothers have lamented the loss of their children. There is nothing in the verse, taken singly, that designates or points out any particular application of it, otherwise than it points to some circumstances which, at the time of writing it, had already happened, and not to a thing yet to happen, for the verse is in the preter or past tense. I go to explain the case and show the application of the verse.

Jeremiah lived in the time that Nebuchadnezar besieged, took, plundered, and destroyed Jerusalem, and led the Jews captive to Babylon. He carried his violence against the Jews to every extreme. He slew the sons of king Zedekiah before his face, he then put out the eyes of Zedekiah, and kept him in prison till the day of his death.

It is of this time of sorrow and suffering to the Jews that Jeremiah is speaking. Their Temple was destroyed, their land desolated, their nation and government entirely broken up, and themselves, men, women and children, carried into captivity. They had too many sorrows of their own, immediately before their eyes, to permit them, or any of their chiefs, to be employing themselves on things that might, or might not, happen in the World seven hundred years afterwards.

It is, as already observed, of this time of sorrow and suffering to the Jews that Jeremiah is speaking in the verse in question. In the next two verses (16, 17), he endeavors to console the sufferers by giving them hopes, and, according to the fashion of speaking in those days, assurances from the Lord, that their sufferings should have an end, and that their children should return again to their own children. But I leave the verses to speak for themselves, and the Old Testament to testify against the New.

Jeremiah xxxi. 15. -- "Thus saith the Lord, a voice was heard in Ramah [it is in the preter tense], lamentation and bitter weeping: Rachel, weeping for her children, refused to be comforted for her children because they were not." Ver. 16, "Thus saith the Lord: Refrain thy voice from weeping, and thine eyes from tears; for thy work shall be rewarded, saith the Lord; and THEY shall come again from the land of the enemy." Ver. 17. -- "And there is hope in thine end, saith the Lord, that thy children shall come again to their own border."

By what strange ignorance or imposition is it, that the children of which Jeremiah speaks, (meaning the people of the Jewish nation, scripturally called children of Israel, and not mere infants under two years old,) and who were to return again from the land of the enemy, and come again into their own borders, can mean the children that Matthew makes Herod to slaughter? Could those return again from the land of the enemy, or how can the land of the enemy be applied to them? Could they come again to their own Borders? Good heavens! How has the world been imposed upon by testament-makers, priestcraft, and pretended prophecies. I pass on to the fifth passage called a prophecy of Jesus Christ.

This, like two of the former, is introduced by dream. Joseph dreamed another dream, and dreameth of another Angel. And Matthew is again the historian of the dream and the dreamer. If it were asked how Matthew could know what Joseph dreamed, neither the Bishop nor all the Church could answer the question. Perhaps it was Matthew that dreamed, and not Joseph; that is, Joseph dreamed by proxy, in Matthew's brain, as they tell us Daniel dreamed for Nebuchadnezar. -- But be this as it may, I go on with my subject.

The account of this dream is in Matthew, ii. 19-23. "But when Herod was dead, behold an Angel of the Lord appeared in a dream to Joseph in Egypt, saying, Arise, and take the young child and his mother and go into the land of Israel; for they are dead which sought the young child's life. And he arose and took the young child and his mother, and came into the land of Israel. But when he heard that Archelaus did reign in Judea in the room of his father Herod, he was afraid to go thither. Notwithstanding being warned of God in a dream [here is another dream] he turned aside into the parts of Galilee; and he came and dwelt in a city called Nazareth, that it might be fulfilled which was spoke by the prophets, He shall be called a Nazarene."

Here is good circumstantial evidence that Matthew dreamed, for there is no such passage in all the Old Testament; and I invite the bishop,[3] and all the priests in Christendom, including those of America, to produce it. I pass on to the sixth passage, called a prophecy of Jesus Christ.

This, as Swift says on another occasion, is lugged in head and shoulders; it need only to be seen in order to be hooted a forced and far-fetched piece of imposition.

Matthew iv. 12-16, "Now when Jesus heard that John was cast into prison, he departed into Galilee: and leaving Nazareth, he came and dwelt in Capernaum, which is upon the sea coast, in the borders of Zebulon and Nephthalim: That it might be fulfilled which was spoken by Esaias [Isaiah] the prophet, saying, 'The land of Zebulon and the land of Nephthalim, by the way of the sea, beyond Jordan, Galilee of the Gentiles, the people which sat in the region and shadow of death, light is springing upon them.'

---

[3] Dr. Watson, Bishop of Llandaff, who had replied to "The Age of Reason." -- Editor.

I wonder Matthew has not made the cris-cross-row, or the Christ-cross-row (I know not how the priests spell it) into a prophecy. He might as well have done this as cut out these unconnected and undescriptive sentences from the place they stand in and dubbed them with that title. The words however, are in Isaiah, ix. 1, 2, as follows: "Nevertheless the dimness shall not be such as was in her vexation, when at the first he lightly afflicted the land of Zebulon and the land of Naphtali, and afterwards did more grievously afflict her by the way of the sea beyond Jordan in Galilee of the nations."

All this relates to two circumstances that had already happened at the time these words in Isaiah were written. The one, where the land of Zebulon and Naphtali had been lightly afflicted, and afterwards more grievously by the way of the sea.

But observe, reader, how Matthew has falsified the text. He begins his quotation at a part of the verse where there is not so much as a comma, and thereby cuts off everything that relates to the first affliction. He then leaves out all that relates to the second affliction, and by this means leaves out every thing that makes the verse intelligible, and reduces it to a senseless skeleton of names of towns.

To bring this imposition of Matthew clearly and immediately before the eye of the reader, I will repeat the verse, and put between crotchets [ ] the words he has left out, and put in Italics those he has preserved.

"[Nevertheless the dimness shall not be such as was in her vexation when at the first he lightly afflicted] the land of Zebulon and the land of Naphtali, [and did afterwards more grievously afflict her] by the way of the sea beyond Jordan in Galilee of the nations."

What gross imposition is it to gut, as the phrase is, a verse in this manner, render it perfectly senseless, and then puff it off on a credulous world as a prophecy. I proceed to the next verse.

Ver. 2. "The people that walked in darkness have seen a great light; they that dwell in the land of the shadow of death, upon them hath the light shined." All this is historical, and not in the least prophetical. The whole is in the preter tense: it speaks of things that had been accomplished at the time the words were written, and not of things to be accomplished afterwards.

As then the passage is in no possible sense prophetical, nor intended to be so, and that to attempt to make it so is not only to falsify the original but to commit a criminal imposition, it is matter of no concern to us, otherwise than as curiosity, to know who the people were of which the passage speaks that sat in darkness, and what the light was that had shined in upon them.

If we look into the preceding chapter, Is. viii., of which ix. is only a continuation, we shall find the writer speaking, at verse 19 of "witches and wizards who peep about and mutter," and of people who made application to them; and he preaches and exhorts them against this darksome practice. It is of this people, and of this darksome practice, of walking in darkness, that he is speaking at ix. 2; and with respect to the light that had shined in upon them, it refers entirely to his own ministry, and to the boldness of it, which opposed itself to that of the witches and wizards who peeped about and muttered.

Isaiah is, upon the whole, a wild disorderly writer, preserving in general no clear chain of perception in the arrangement of his ideas, and consequently producing no defined conclusions from them. It is the wildness of his stile, the confusion of his ideas, and the ranting metaphors he employs, that have afforded so many opportunities to priestcraft in some cases, and to superstition in others, to impose those defects upon the world as prophecies of Jesus Christ. Finding no direct meaning in them, and not knowing what to make of them, and supposing at the same time they were intended to have a meaning, they supplied the defect by inventing a meaning of their own, and called it 'his.' I have however in this place done Isaiah the justice to rescue him from the claws of Matthew, who has torn him unmercifully to pieces, and from the imposition or ignorance of priests and commentators, by letting Isaiah speak for himself.

If the words walking in darkness, and light breaking in, could in any case be applied prophetically, which they cannot be, they would better apply to the times we now live in than to any other. The world has "walked in darkness" for eighteen hundred years, both as to religion and government, and it is only since the American Revolution began that light has broken in. The belief of one God, whose attributes are revealed to us in the book or scripture of the creation, which no human hand can counterfeit or falsify, and not in the written or printed book which, as Matthew has shown, can be altered or falsified by ignorance or design, is now making its way among us: and as to government, 'the light is already gone forth,' and whilst men ought to be careful not to be blinded by the excess of it, as at a certain time in France when everything was Robespierrean violence, they ought to reverence, and even to adore it, with all the perseverance that true wisdom can inspire.

I pass on to the seventh passage, called a prophecy of Jesus Christ.

Matthew viii. 16, 17. "When the evening was come, they brought unto him [Jesus] many that were possessed with devils, and he cast out the spirits with his word, and healed all that were sick: That it might be fulfilled which was spoken by Esaias (Isaiah) the prophet, saying, himself took our infirmities, and bare our sickness."

This affair of people being possessed by devils, and of casting them out, was the fable of the day when the books of the New Testament were written. It had not existence at any other time. The books of the Old Testament mention no such thing; the people of the present day know of no such thing; nor does the history of any people or country speak of such a thing. It starts upon us all at once in the book of Matthew, and is altogether an invention of the New Testament-makers and the Christian church. The book of Matthew is the first book where the word Devil is mentioned.[4] We read in some of the books of the Old Testament of things called familiar spirits, the supposed companions of people called witches and wizards. It was no other than the trick of pretended conjurers to obtain money from credulous and ignorant people, or the fabricated charge of superstitious malignancy against unfortunate and decrepit old age. But the idea of a familiar spirit, if we can affix any idea to the term, is exceedingly different to that of being possessed by a devil. In the one case, the supposed familiar spirit is a dexterous agent, that comes and goes and does as he is bidden; in the other, he is a turbulent roaring monster, that tears and tortures the body into convulsions. Reader, whoever thou art, put thy trust in thy

---

[4] The word devil is a personification of the word evil. -- Author.

creator, make use of the reason he endowed thee with, and cast from thee all such fables.

The passage alluded to by Matthew, for as a quotation it is false, is in Isaiah, Iiii. 4, which is as follows: "Surely he [the person of whom Isaiah is speaking] hath borne our griefs and carried our sorrows." It is in the preter tense.

Here is nothing about casting out devils, nor curing of sicknesses. The passage, therefore, so far from being a prophecy of Christ, is not even applicable as a circumstance.

Isaiah, or at least the writer of the book that bears his name, employs the whole of this chapter, Iiii., in lamenting the sufferings of some deceased persons, of whom he speaks very pathetically. It is a monody on the death of a friend; but he mentions not the name of the person, nor gives any circumstance of him by which he can be personally known; and it is this silence, which is evidence of nothing, that Matthew has laid hold of, to put the name of Christ to it; as if the chiefs of the Jews, whose sorrows were then great, and the times they lived in big with danger, were never thinking about their own affairs, nor the fate of their own friends, but were continually running a Wild-Goose chase into futurity.

To make a monody into a prophecy is an absurdity. The characters and circumstances of men, even in the different ages of the world, are so much alike, that what is said of one may with propriety be said of many; but this fitness does not make the passage into a prophecy; and none but an impostor, or a bigot, would call it so.

Isaiah, in deploring the hard fate and loss of his friend, mentions nothing of him but what the human lot of man is subject to. All the cases he states of him, his persecutions, his imprisonment, his patience in suffering, and his perseverance in principle, are all within the line of nature; they belong exclusively to none, and may with justness be said of many. But if Jesus Christ was the person the church represents him to be, that which would exclusively apply to him must be something that could not apply to any other person; something beyond the line of nature, something beyond the lot of mortal man; and there are no such expressions in this chapter, nor any other chapter in the Old Testament.

It is no exclusive description to say of a person, as is said of the person Isaiah is lamenting in this chapter, He was oppressed and he was afflicted, yet he opened not his mouth; he is brought as a Lamb to the slaughter, and as a sheep before his shearers is dumb, so he openeth not his mouth. This may be said of thousands of persons, who have suffered oppressions and unjust death with patience, silence, and perfect resignation.

Grotius, whom the Bishop [of Llandaff] esteems a most learned man, and who certainly was so, supposes that the person of whom Isaiah is speaking, is Jeremiah. Grotius is led into this opinion from the agreement there is between the description given by Isaiah and the case of Jeremiah, as stated in the book that bears his name. If Jeremiah was an innocent man, and not a traitor in the interest of Nebuchadnezar when Jerusalem was besieged, his case was hard; he was accused by his countrymen, was persecuted, oppressed, and imprisoned, and he says of himself, (see Jer. xi. 19,) "But as for me, I was like a lamb or an ox that is brought to the slaughter."

I should be inclined to the same opinion with Grotius, had Isaiah lived at the time when Jeremiah underwent the cruelties of which he speaks; but Isaiah died about fifty years before; and it is of a person of his own time whose case Isaiah is lamenting in the chapter in question, and which imposition and bigotry, more than seven hundred years afterwards, perverted into a prophecy of a person they call Jesus Christ.

I pass on to the eighth passage called a prophecy of Jesus Christ.

Matthew xii. 14-21: "Then the Pharisees went out and held a council against him, how they might destroy him. But when Jesus knew it he withdrew himself; and great numbers followed him and he healed them all; and he charged them they should not make him known: That it might be fulfilled which was spoken by Esaias (Isaiah) the prophet, saying, Behold my servant, whom I have chosen; my beloved, in whom my soul is well pleased; I will put my spirit upon him, and he shall shew judgment to the Gentiles. He shall not strive nor cry; neither shall any man hear his voice in the streets. A bruised reed shall he not break, and smocking flax shall he not quench, till he send forth judgment unto victory. And in his name shall the Gentiles trust."

In the first place, this passage hath not the least relation to the purpose for which it is quoted.

Matthew says, that the Pharisees held a council against Jesus to destroy him -- that Jesus withdrew himself -- that great numbers followed him -- that he healed them -- and that he charged them they should not make him known. But the passage Matthew has quoted as being fulfilled by these circumstances does not so much as apply to any one of them. It has nothing to do with the Pharisees holding a council to destroy Jesus -- with his withdrawing himself -- with great numbers following him -- with his healing them -- nor with his charging them not to make him known.

The purpose for which the passage is quoted, and the passage itself, are as remote from each other, as nothing from something. But the case is, that people have been so long in the habit of reading the books called the Bible and Testament with their eyes shut, and their senses locked up, that the most stupid inconsistencies have passed on them for truth, and imposition for prophecy. The all-wise creator hath been dishonored by being made the author of Fable, and the human mind degraded by believing it.

In this passage, as in that last mentioned, the name of the person of whom the passage speaks is not given, and we are left in the dark respecting him. It is this defect in the history that bigotry and imposition have laid hold of, to call It prophecy.

Had Isaiah lived in the time of Cyrus, the passage would descriptively apply to him. As king of Persia, his authority was great among the Gentiles, and it is of such a character the passage speaks; and his friendship for the Jews, whom he liberated from captivity, and who might then be compared to a bruised reed, was extensive. But this description does not apply to Jesus Christ, who had no authority among the Gentiles; and as to his own countrymen, figuratively described by the bruised reed, it was they who crucified him. Neither can it be said of him that he did not cry, and that his voice was not heard in the street. As a preacher it was his business to be heard, and we are told that he traveled about the country for that purpose. Matthew has given a long sermon, which (if his authority is good, but which is much to be doubted since he imposes so much,) Jesus preached to a multitude upon a mountain, and it would be a quibble to say that a mountain is not a street, since it is a place equally as public.

The last verse in the passage (the 4th) as it stands in Isaiah, and which Matthew has not quoted, says, "He shall not fail nor be discouraged till he have set judgment in the Earth and the Isles shall wait for his law." This also applies to Cyrus. He was not discouraged, he did not fail, he conquered all Babylon, liberated the Jews, and established laws. But this cannot be said of Jesus Christ, who in the passage before us, according to Matthew, [xii. 15], withdrew himself for fear of the Pharisees, and charged the people that followed him not to make it known where he was; and who, according to other parts of the Testament, was continually moving from place to place to avoid being apprehended.[5]

---

[5] In the second part of the 'Age of Reason,' I have shown that the book ascribed to Isaiah is not only miscellaneous as to matter, but as to authorship; that there are parts in it which could not be written by Isaiah, because they speak of things one hundred and fifty years after he was dead. The instance I have given of this, in that work, corresponds with the subject I am upon, at least a little better than Matthew's introduction and his question.

Isaiah lived, the latter part of his life, in the time of Hezekiah, and it was about one hundred and fifty years from the death of Hezekiah to the first year of the reign of Cyrus, when Cyrus published a proclamation, which is given in Ezra i., for the return of the Jews to Jerusalem. It cannot be doubted, at least it ought not to be doubted, that the Jews would feel an affectionate gratitude for this act of benevolent justice, and it is natural they would express that gratitude in the customary stile, bombastic and hyperbolical as it was, which they used on extraordinary occasions, and which was and still is in practice with all the eastern nations.

The instance to which I refer, and which is given in the second part of the Age of Reason, Is. xliv. 28 and xlv. 1, in these words: "That saith of Cyrus, he is my shepherd and shall perform all my pleasure: even saying to Jerusalem, Thou shalt be built, and to the Temple, Thy foundation shall be laid. Thus saith the Lard to his anointed, to Cyrus, whose right hand I have holden to subdue nations before him; and I will loose the loins of kings, to open before him the two-leaved gates, and the gates shall not be shut."

This complimentary address is in the present tense, which shows that the things of which it speaks were in existence at the time of writing it; and consequently that the author must have been at least one hundred and fifty years later than Isaiah, and that the book which bears his name is a compilation. The Proverbs called Solomon's, and the Psalms called David's, are of the same kind. The last two verses of the second book of Chronicles, and the first three verses of Ezra i. are word for word the same; which show that the compilers of the Bible mixed the writings of different authors together, and put them under some common head.

As we have here an instance in Isaiah xliv. and xlv. of the introduction of the name of Cyrus into a book to which it cannot belong, it affords good ground to

But it is immaterial to us, at this distance of time, to know who the person was: it is sufficient to the purpose I am upon, that of detecting fraud and falsehood, to know who it was not, and to show it was not the person called Jesus Christ.

I pass on to the ninth passage called a prophecy of Jesus Christ.

Matthew xxi. 1-5. "And when they drew nigh unto Jerusalem, and were come to Bethphage, unto the mount of Olives, then Jesus sent two of his disciples, saying unto them, Go into the village over against you, and straightway ye shall find an Ass tied, and a colt with her; loose them and bring them unto me. And if any man say ought to you, ye shall say, the Lord hath need of them, and straightway he will send them. All this was done that it might be fulfilled which was spoken by the prophet, saying, Tell ye the daughter of Sion, Behold thy King cometh unto thee, meek, and sitting upon an Ass, and a colt the foal of an Ass."

Poor ass! let it be some consolation amidst all thy sufferings, that if the heathen world erected a Bear into a constellation, the Christian world has elevated thee into a prophecy.

---

conclude, that the passage in chapter xlii., in which the character of Cyrus is given without his name, has been introduced in like manner, and that the person there spoken of is Cyrus. -- Author.

This passage is in Zechariah ix. 9, and is one of the whims of friend Zechariah to congratulate his countrymen, who were then returning from captivity in Babylon, and himself with them, to Jerusalem. It has no concern with any other subject. It is strange that apostles, priests, and commentators, never permit, or never suppose, the Jews to be speaking of their own affairs. Every thing in the Jewish books is perverted and distorted into meanings never intended by the writers. Even the poor ass must not be a Jew-ass but a Christian-ass. I wonder they did not make an apostle of him, or a bishop, or at least make him speak and prophesy. He could have lifted up his voice as loud as any of them.

Zechariah, in the first chapter of his book, indulges himself in several whims on the joy of getting back to Jerusalem. He says at the 8th verse, "I saw by night [Zechariah was a sharp-sighted seer] and behold a man setting on a red horse, [yes reader, a red horse,] and he stood among the myrtle trees that were in the bottom, and behind him were red horses, speckled and white." He says nothing about green horses, nor blue horses, perhaps because it is difficult to distinguish green from blue by night, but a Christian can have no doubt they were there, because "faith is the evidence of things not seen."

Zechariah then introduces an angel among his horses, but he does not tell us what color the angel was of, whether black or white, nor whether he came to buy horses, or only to look at them as curiosities, for certainly they were of that kind. Be this however as it may, he enters into conversation with this angel on the joyful affair of getting back to Jerusalem, and he saith at the 16th verse, "Therefore, thus saith the Lord, I AM RETURNED to Jerusalem with mercies; my house shall be built in it saith the Lord of hosts, and a line shall be stretched forth upon Jerusalem." An expression signifying the rebuilding the city.

All this, whimsical and imaginary as it is, sufficiently proves that it was the entry of the Jews into Jerusalem from captivity, and not the entry of Jesus Christ seven hundred years afterwards, that is the subject upon which Zechariah is always speaking.

As to the expression of riding upon an ass, which commentators represent as a sign of humility in Jesus Christ, the case is, he never was so well mounted before. The asses of those countries are large and well proportioned, and were anciently the chief of riding animals. Their beasts of burden, and which served also for the conveyance of the poor, were camels and dromedaries. We read in Judges X. 4, that Jair [one of the judges of Israel] "had thirty sons that rode on thirty ass-colts, and they had thirty cities." But commentators distort every thing.

There is besides very reasonable grounds to conclude that this story of Jesus riding publicly into Jerusalem, accompanied, as it is said at verses 8 and 9, by a great multitude, shouting and rejoicing and spreading their garments by the way, is a story altogether destitute of truth.

In the last passage called a prophecy that I examined, Jesus is represented as withdrawing, that is, running away, and concealing himself for fear of being apprehended, and charging the people that were with him not to make him known. No new circumstance had arisen in the interim to change his condition for the better; yet here he is represented as making his public entry into the same city from which he had fled for safety. The two cases contradict each other so much, that if both are not false, one of them at least can scarcely be true. For my own part, I do not believe there is one word of historical truth in the whole book. I look upon it at best to be a romance: the principal personage of which is an imaginary or allegorical character founded upon some tale, and in which the moral is in many parts good, and the narrative part very badly and blunderingly written.

I pass on to the tenth passage called a prophecy of Jesus Christ.

Matthew xxvi. 51-56: "And behold one of them which was with Jesus [meaning Peter] stretched out his hand, and drew his sword, and struck a servant of the high priest, and smote off his ear. Then said Jesus unto him, put up again thy sword into its place: for all they that take the sword shall perish with the sword.

Thinkest thou that I cannot now pray to my Father, and he shall presently give me more than twelve legions of angels? But how then shall the scriptures be fulfilled that thus it must be? In that same hour Jesus said to the multitudes, Are ye come out as against a thief, with swords and with staves for to take me? I sat daily with you teaching in the temple, and ye laid no hold on me. But all this was done that the scriptures of the prophets might be fulfilled."

This loose and general manner of speaking, admits neither of detection nor of proof. Here is no quotation given, nor the name of any bible author mentioned, to which reference can be had.

There are, however, some high improbabilities against the truth of the account.

First -- It is not probable that the Jews, who were then a conquered people, and under subjection to the Romans, should be permitted to wear swords.

Secondly -- If Peter had attacked the servant of the high priest and cut off his ear, he would have been immediately taken up by the guard that took up his master and sent to prison with him.

Thirdly -- What sort of disciples and preaching apostles must those of Christ have been that wore swords?

Fourthly -- This scene is represented to have taken place the same evening of what is called the Lord's supper, which makes, according to the ceremony of it, the inconsistency of wearing swords the greater.

I pass on to the eleventh passage called a prophecy of Jesus Christ.

Matthew xxvii. 3-10: "Then Judas, which had betrayed him, when he saw that he was condemned, repented himself, and brought again the thirty pieces of silver to the chief priests and elders, saying, I have sinned in that I have betrayed the innocent blood. And they said, What is that to us, see thou to that. And he cast down the thirty pieces of silver, and departed, and went and hanged himself. And the chief priests took the silver pieces and said, it is not lawful to put them in the treasury, because it is the price of blood. And they took counsel, and bought with them the potter's field, to bury strangers in. Wherefore that field is called the field of blood unto this day. Then was fulfilled that which was spoken by Jeremiah the prophet, saying, And they took the thirty pieces of silver, the price of him that was valued, whom they of the children of Israel did value, and gave them for the potter's field, as the Lord appointed me."

This is a most barefaced piece of imposition. The passage in Jeremiah which speaks of the purchase of a field, has no more to do with the case to which Matthew applies it, than it has to do with the purchase of lands in America. I will recite the whole passage:

Jeremiah xxxii. 6-15: "And Jeremiah said, The word of the Lord came unto me, saying, Behold Hanameel, the son of Shallum thine uncle, shall come unto thee, saying, Buy thee my field that is in Anathoth, for the right of redemption is thine to buy it. So Hanameel mine uncle's son came to me in the court of the prison, according to the word of the Lord, and said unto me, Buy my field I pray thee that is in Anathoth, which is in the country of Benjamin; for the right of inheritance is thine, and the redemption is thine; buy it for thyself. Then I knew this was the word of the Lord. And I bought the field of Hanameel mine uncle's son, that was in Anathoth, and weighed him the money, even seventeen shekels of silver. And I subscribed the evidence and sealed it, and took witnesses and weighed him the money in the balances. So I took the evidence of the purchase, both that which was sealed according to the law and custom, and that which was open; and I gave the evidence of the purchase unto Baruch the son of Neriah, the son of Maaseiah, in the sight of Hanameel mine uncle's son, and in the presence of the witnesses that subscribed [the book of the purchase,] before all the Jews that sat in the court of the prison. And I charged Baruch before them, saying, Thus saith the Lord of hosts, the God of Israel: Take these evidences, this evidence of the purchase, both which is sealed, and this evidence which is open, and put them in an earthen vessel, that they may continue many days. For thus saith the Lord of hosts, the God of Israel: Houses and fields and vineyards shall be possessed again in this land."

I forbear making any remark on this abominable imposition of Matthew. The thing glaringly speaks for itself. It is priests and commentators that I rather ought to censure, for having preached falsehood so long, and kept people in darkness with respect to those impositions. I am not contending with these men upon points of doctrine, for I know that sophistry has always a city of refuge. I am speaking of facts; for wherever the thing called a fact is a falsehood, the faith founded upon it is delusion, and the doctrine raised upon it not true. Ah, reader, put thy trust in thy creator, and thou wilt be safe; but if thou trustest to the book called the scriptures thou trustest to the rotten staff of fable and falsehood. But I return to my subject.

There is among the whims and reveries of Zechariah, mention made of thirty pieces of silver given to a Potter. They can hardly have been so stupid as to mistake a potter for a field: and if they had, the passage in Zechariah has no more to do with Jesus, Judas, and the field to bury strangers in, than that already quoted. I will recite the passage.

Zechariah xi. 7-14: "And I will feed the flock of slaughter, even you, O poor of the flock. And I took unto me two staves; the one I called Beauty, and the other I called Bands; and I fed the flock.

Three shepherds also I cut off in one month; and my soul loathed them, and their soul also abhorred me. Then said I, I will not feed you; that which dieth, let it die; and that which is to be cut off, let it be cut off; and let the rest eat every one the flesh of another. -- And I took my staff, even Beauty, and cut it asunder, that I might break my covenant which I had made with all the people. And it was broken in that day; and so the poor of the flock who waited upon me knew that it was the word of the Lord. And I said unto them, If ye think good, give me my price, and if not, forbear. So they weighed for my price thirty pieces of silver. And the Lord said unto me, Cast it unto the potter; a goodly price that I was prised at of them. And I took the thirty pieces of silver, and cast them to the potter in the house of the Lord. Then I cut asunder mine other staff, even Bands, that I might break the brotherhood between Judah and Israel."[6]

---

[6] Whiston, in his Essay on the Old Testament, says, that the passage of Zechariah of which I have spoken, was, in the copies of the Bible of the first century, in the book of Jeremiah, from whence, says he, it was taken and inserted without coherence in that of Zechariah. Well, let it be so, it does not make the case a whit the better for the New Testament; but it makes the case a great deal the worse for the Old. Because it shows, as I have mentioned respecting some passages in a book ascribed to Isaiah, that the works of different authors have been so mixed and confounded together, they cannot now be discriminated, except where they are historical, chronological, or biographical, as in the interpolation in Isaiah. It is the name of Cyrus, inserted

There is no making either head or tail of this incoherent gibberish. His two staves, one called Beauty and the other Bands, is so much like a fairy tale, that I doubt if it had any other origin. There is, however, no part that has the least relation to the case stated in Matthew; on the contrary, it is the reverse of it. Here the thirty Pieces of silver, whatever it was for, is called a goodly price,

---

where it could not be inserted, as he was not in existence till one hundred and fifty years after the time of Isaiah, that detects the interpolation and the blunder with it.

Whiston was a man of great literary learning, and what is of much higher degree, of deep scientific learning. He was one of the best and most celebrated mathematicians of his time, for which he was made professor of mathematics of the University of Cambridge. He wrote so much in defense of the Old Testament, and of what he calls prophecies of Jesus Christ, that at last he began to suspect the truth of the Scriptures, and wrote against them; for it is only those who examine them, that see the imposition. Those who believe them most, are those who know least about them.

Whiston, after writing so much in defense of the Scriptures, was at last prosecuted for writing against them. It was this that gave occasion to Swift, in his ludicrous epigram on Ditton and Whiston, each of which set up to find out the longitude, to call the one good master Ditton and the other wicked Will Whiston. But as Swift was a great associate with the Freethinkers of those days, such as Bolingbroke, Pope, and others, who did not believe the book called the scriptures, there is no certainty whether he wittily called him wicked for defending the scriptures, or for writing against them. The known character of Swift decides for the former. -- Author.

43

it was as much as the thing was worth, and according to the language of the day, was approved of by the Lord, and the money given to the potter in the house of the Lord. In the case of Jesus and Judas, as stated in Matthew, the thirty pieces of silver were the price of blood; the transaction was condemned by the Lord, and the money when refunded was refused admittance into the Treasury. Every thing in the two cases is the reverse of each other.

Besides this, a very different and direct contrary account to that of Matthew, is given of the affair of Judas, in the book called the Acts of the Apostles; according to that book the case is, that so far from Judas repenting and returning the money, and the high priest buying a field with it to bury strangers in, Judas kept the money and bought a field with it for himself; and instead of hanging himself as Matthew says, that he fell headlong and burst asunder. Some commentators endeavor to get over one part of the contradiction by ridiculously supposing that Judas hanged himself first and the rope broke.

Acts i. 16-18: "Men and brethren, this scripture must needs have been fulfilled which the Holy Ghost by the mouth of David spoke before concerning Judas, which was guide to them that took Jesus, [David says not a word about Judas,] for he [Judas] was numbered among us and obtained part of our ministry. Now this man purchased a field with the reward of iniquity, and falling

44

headlong, he burst asunder in the midst and his bowels gushed out."

Is it not a species of blasphemy to call the New Testament revealed religion, when we see in it such contradictions and absurdities? I pass on to the twelfth passage called a prophecy of Jesus Christ.

Matthew xxvii. 35. "And they crucified him, and parted his garments, casting lots; that it might be fulfilled which was spoken by the prophet, They parted my garments among them, and upon my vesture did they cast lots." This expression is in Psalm xxii. 18. The writer of that Psalm (who-ever he was, for the Psalms are a collection and not the work of one man) is speaking of himself and his own case, and not that of another. He begins this Psalm with the words which the New Testament writers ascribed to Jesus Christ: "My God, my God, why hast thou forsaken me" -- words which might be uttered by a complaining man without any great impropriety, but very improperly from the mouth of a reputed God.

The picture which the writer draws of his own situation, in this Psalm, is gloomy enough. He is not prophesying, but complaining of his own hard case. He represents himself as surrounded by enemies and beset by persecutions of every kind; and by way of showing the inveteracy of his persecutors he says,

"They parted my garments among them, and cast lots upon my vesture." The expression is in the present tense; and is the same as to say, they pursue me even to the clothes upon my back, and dispute how they shall divide them. Besides, the word vesture does not always mean clothing of any kind, but property, or rather the admitting a man to, or investing him with property; and as it is used in this Psalm distinct from the word garment, it appears to be used in this sense. But Jesus had no property; for they make him say of himself, "The foxes have holes and the birds of the air have nests, but the Son of Man hath not where to lay his head."

But be this as it may, if we permit ourselves to suppose the Almighty would condescend to tell, by what is called the spirit of prophecy, what could come to pass in some future age of the world, it is an injury to our own faculties, and to our ideas of his greatness, to imagine that it would be about an old coat, or an old pair of breeches, or about any thing which the common accidents of life, or the quarrels which attend it, exhibit every day.

That which is in the power of man to do, or in his will not to do, is not a subject for prophecy, even if there were such a thing, because it cannot carry with it any evidence of divine power, or divine interposition. The ways of God are not the ways of men. That which an almighty power performs, or wills, is not within the circle of human power to do, or to control. But any executioner and his assistants might quarrel about dividing the

46

garments of a sufferer, or divide them without quarrelling, and by that means fulfill the thing called a prophecy, or set it aside.

In the passages before examined, I have exposed the falsehood of them. In this I exhibit its degrading meanness, as an insult to the creator and an injury to human reason.

Here end the passages called prophecies by Matthew.

Matthew concludes his book by saying, that when Christ expired on the cross, the rocks rent, the graves opened, and the bodies of many of the saints arose; and Mark says, there was darkness over the land from the sixth hour until the ninth. They produce no prophecy for this; but had these things been facts, they would have been a proper subject for prophecy, because none but an almighty power could have inspired a fore-knowledge of them, and afterwards fulfilled them. Since then there is no such prophecy, but a pretended prophecy of an old coat, the proper deduction is, there were no such things, and that the book of Matthew was fable and falsehood.

I pass on to the book called the Gospel according to St. Mark.

THE BOOK OF MARK

There are but few passages in Mark called prophecies; and but few in Luke and John. Such as there are I shall examine, and also such other passages as interfere with those cited by Matthew.

Mark begins his book by a passage which he puts in the shape of a prophecy. Mark i. 1,2. "The beginning of the Gospel of Jesus Christ, the Son of God; As it is written in the prophets, Behold I send my messenger before thy face, which shall prepare thy way before thee." (Malachi iii. 1.) The passage in the original is in the first person. Mark makes this passage to be a prophecy of John the Baptist, said by the Church to be a forerunner of Jesus Christ. But if we attend to the verses that follow this expression, as it stands in Malachi, and to the first and fifth verses of the next chapter, we shall see that this application of it is erroneous and false.

Malachi having said, at the first verse, "Behold I will send my messenger, and he shall prepare the way before me," says, at the second verse, "But who may abide the day of his coming? And who shall stand when he appeareth? For he is like a refiner's fire, and like fuller's soap." This description can have no reference to the birth of Jesus Christ, and consequently none to John the Baptist. It is a scene of fear and terror that is here described, and the birth of Christ is always spoken of as a time of joy and glad tidings.

Malachi, continuing to speak on the same subject, explains in the next chapter what the scene is of which he speaks in the verses above quoted, and whom the person is whom he calls the messenger.

"Behold," says he, (iv. 1,) "the day cometh that shall burn like an oven, and all the proud, yea, and all that do wickedly, shall be stubble; and the day cometh that shall burn them up, saith the Lord of hosts, that it shall leave them neither root nor branch." Verse 5. "Behold I will send you Elijah the prophet before the coming of the great and dreadful day of the Lord."

By what right, or by what imposition or ignorance Mark has made Elijah into John the Baptist, and Malachi's description of the day of judgment into the birth day of Christ, I leave to the Bishop [of Llandaff] to settle.

Mark, (i. 2,3), confounds two passages together, taken from different books of the Old Testament. The second verse, "Behold I send my messenger before thy face, which shall prepare thy way before thee," is taken, as I have said before, from Malachi. The third verse, which says, "The voice of one crying in the wilderness, Prepare ye the way of the Lord, make his paths straight," is not in Malachi, but in Isaiah, xl. 3, Whiston says that both these verses were originally in Isaiah. If so, it is another instance of the disordered state of the Bible, and corroborates what I have said with respect to the name and description of Cyrus being in the book of Isaiah, to which it cannot chronologically belong.

The words in Isaiah, -- "The voice of him that cryeth in the wilderness, Prepare ye the way of the Lord, make his Paths straight," -- are in the present tense, and consequently not predictive. It is one of those rhetorical figures which the Old Testament authors frequently used. That it is merely rhetorical and metaphorical, may be seen at the 6th verse: "And the voice said, cry; and he said what shall I cry? All flesh is grass." This is evidently nothing but a figure; for flesh is not grass otherwise than as a figure or metaphor, where one thing is put for another. Besides which, the whole passage is too general and too declamatory to be applied exclusively to any particular person or purpose.

I pass onto the eleventh chapter.

In this chapter, Mark speaks of Christ riding into Jerusalem upon a colt, but he does not make it the accomplishment of a prophecy, as Matthew has done, for he says nothing about a prophecy. Instead of which he goes on the other tack, and in order to add new honors to the ass, he makes it to be a miracle; for he says, ver. 2, it was a colt "whereon never man sat;" signifying thereby, that as the ass had not been broken, he consequently was inspired into good manners, for we do not hear that he kicked Jesus Christ off. There is not a word about his kicking in all the four Evangelists.

I pass on from these feats of horsemanship performed upon a jack-ass, to the 15th chapter. At the 24th verse of this chapter Mark speaks of parting Christ's garments and casting lots upon them, but he applies no prophecy to it as Matthew does. He rather speaks of it as a thing then in practice with executioners, as it is at this day.

At the 28th verse of the same chapter, Mark speaks of Christ being crucified between two thieves; that, says he, the scripture might be fulfilled, "which saith, and he was numbered with the transgressors." The same might be said of the thieves.

This expression is in Isaiah liii. 12. Grotius applies it to Jeremiah. But the case has happened so often in the world, where innocent men have been numbered with transgressors, and is still continually happening, that it is absurdity to call it a prophecy of any particular person. All those whom the church calls martyrs were numbered with transgressors. All the honest patriots who fell upon the scaffold in France, in the time of Robespierre, were numbered with transgressors; and if himself had not fallen, the same case according to a note in his own handwriting, had befallen me;[7] yet I suppose the Bishop [of Llandaff] will not allow that Isaiah was prophesying of Thomas Paine.

These are all the passages in Mark which have any reference to prophecies.

Mark concludes his book by making Jesus to say to his disciples, (xvi. 16-18), "Go ye into all the world and preach the Gospel to every creature; he that believeth and is baptized shall be saved, but he that believeth not shall be damned, [fine popish stuff this,] and these signs shall follow them that believe: in my name they shall cast out devils; they shall speak with new tongues; they shall take up serpents; and if they drink any deadly thing it shall not hurt them; they shall lay hands on the sick, and they shall recover."[8]

Now, the Bishop, in order to know if he has all this saving and wonder-working faith, should try those things upon himself. He should take a good dose of arsenic, and if he please, I will send him a rattle-snake from America.

---

[7] See vol. iii. p. 222 of this edition of Paine's Writings; also Preface to Part of "The Age of Reason" -- Editor.

[8] These are among the twelve apocryphal verses added to Mark. -- Editor.

As for myself, as I believe in God and not at all in Jesus Christ, nor in the books called the scriptures, the experiment does not concern me.

I pass on to the book of Luke.

THE BOOK OF LUKE

There are no passages in Luke called prophecies, excepting those which relate to the passages I have already examined.

Luke speaks of Mary being espoused to Joseph, but he makes no references to the passage in Isaiah, as Matthew does. He speaks also of Jesus riding into Jerusalem upon a colt, but he says nothing about a prophecy. He speaks of John the baptist and refers to the passage in Isaiah of which I have already spoken.

At chapter xiii. 31, 32, he says, "The same day there came certain of the Pharisees, saying unto him [Jesus] Get thee out and depart hence, for Herod will kill thee. And he said unto them, Go ye and tell that fox, Behold I cast out devils, and I do cures to- day and to-morrow, and the third day I shall be Perfected.

Matthew makes Herod to die whilst Christ was a child in Egypt, and makes Joseph to return with the child on the news of Herod's death, who had sought to kill him. Luke makes Herod to be living, and to seek the life of Jesus after Jesus was thirty years of age: for he says, (iii. 23), "And Jesus began to be about thirty years of age, being, as was supposed, the son of Joseph."

The obscurity in which the historical part of the New Testament is involved, with respect to Herod, may afford to priests and commentators a plea, which to some may appear plausible, but to none satisfactory, that the Herod of which Matthew speaks, and the Herod of which Luke speaks, were different persons. Matthew calls Herod a king; and Luke (iii. 1) calls Herod Tetrarch (that is, Governor) of Galilee. But there could be no such person as a king Herod, because the Jews and their country were then under the dominion of the Roman Emperors who governed then by Tetrarchs, or Governors.

Luke ii. makes Jesus to be born when Cyrenius was Governor of Syria, to which government Judea was annexed; and according to this, Jesus was not born in the time of Herod. Luke says nothing about Herod seeking the life of Jesus when he was born; nor of his destroying the children under two years old; nor of Joseph fleeing with Jesus into Egypt; nor of his returning from thence. On the contrary, the book of Luke speaks as if the person it calls Christ had never been out of Judea, and that Herod sought his life after he commenced preaching, as is before stated. I have already shown that Luke, in the book called the Acts of the Apostles, (which commentators ascribe to Luke,) contradicts the account in Matthew with respect to Judas and the thirty pieces of silver. Matthew says that Judas returned the money, and that the high priests bought with it a field to bury strangers in; Luke says that Judas kept the money, and bought a field with it for himself.

As it is impossible the wisdom of God should err, so it is impossible those books should have been written by divine inspiration. Our belief in God and his unerring wisdom forbids us to believe it. As for myself, I feel religiously happy in the total disbelief of it.

There are no other passages called prophecies in Luke than those I have spoken of. I pass on to the book of John.

THE BOOK OF JOHN

John, like Mark and Luke, is not much of a prophecy-monger. He speaks of the ass, and the casting lots for Jesus's clothes, and some other trifles, of which I have already spoken.

John makes Jesus to say, (v. 46), "For had ye believed Moses, ye would have believed me, for he wrote of me." The book of the Acts, in speaking of Jesus says, (iii. 22), "For Moses truly said unto the fathers, A prophet shall the Lord your God raise up unto you of your brethren, like unto me; him shall ye hear in all things whatsoever he shall say unto you."

This passage is in Deuteronomy, xviii. 15. They apply it as a prophecy of Jesus. What imposition! The person spoken of in Deuteronomy, and also in Numbers, where the same person is spoken of, is Joshua, the minister of Moses, and his immediate successor, and just such another Robespierrean character as Moses is represented to have been. The case, as related in those books, is as follows:

Moses was grown old and near to his end, and in order to prevent confusion after his death, for the Israelites had no settled system of government, it was thought best to nominate a successor to Moses whilst he was yet living. This was done, as we are told, in the following manner: Numbers xxvii. 12,13: "And the Lord said unto Moses, Get thee up into this mount Abarim, and see the land which I have given unto the children of Israel. And when thou hast seen it thou also shalt be gathered unto thy people, as Aaron thy brother is gathered." Ver. I 5-20. "And Moses spoke unto the Lord, saying, Let the Lord, the God of the spirits of all flesh, set a man over the congregation, which may go out before them, and which may go in before them, and which may lead them out, and which may bring them in; that the congregation of the Lord be not as sheep that have no shepherd. And the Lord said unto Moses, take thee Joshua, the son of Nun, a man in whom is the spirit, and lay thine hand upon him; and set him before Eleazar the priest, and before all the congregation; and give him a charge in their sight. And thou shalt put some of thine honor upon him, that all the congregation of the children of Israel may be obedient." Ver. 22, 23. "And Moses did as the Lord commanded him; and he took Joshua, and set him before Eleazar the priest, and before all the congregation; and he laid hands upon him, and gave him a charge, as the Lord commanded by the hand of Moses."

I have nothing to do, in this place, with the truth, or the conjuration here practiced, of raising up a successor to Moses like unto himself. The passage sufficiently proves it is Joshua, and that it is an imposition in John to make the case into a prophecy of Jesus. But the prophecy-mangers were so inspired with falsehood, that they never speak truth.[9]

---

[9] Newton, Bishop of Bristol in England, published a work in three volumes, entitled, "Dissertations on the Prophecies." The work is tediously written and tiresome to read. He strains hard to make every passage into a prophecy that suits his purpose. Among others, be makes this expression of Moses, "the Lord shall raise thee up a prophet like unto me," into a prophecy of Christ, who was not born, according to the Bible chronologies, till fifteen hundred and fifty-two years after the time of Moses; whereas it was an immediate successor to Moses, who was then near his end, that is spoken of in the passage above quoted. This Bishop, the better to impose this passage on the world as a prophecy of Christ, has entirely omitted the account in the book of Numbers which I have given at length, word for word, and which shows, beyond the possibility of a doubt, that the person spoken of by Moses is Joshua, find no other person. Newton is but a superficial writer. He takes up things upon hear-say, and inserts them without either examination or reflection, and the more extraordinary and incredible they are, the better be likes them. In speaking of the walls of Babylon, (vol. i. p. 263,) he makes a quotation from a traveler of the name of Tavernaer, whom he calls, (by way of giving credit to what he says,) a celebrated traveler, that those walls were made of burnt brick, ten feet square and three feet thick. If Newton had only thought of calculating the weight of such a brick, he would have seen the impossibility of their being used or even made. A brick ten feet square, and three feet thick, contains 300 cubic feet, and allowing a cubic foot of brick to be only one hundred pounds, each of the Bishop's bricks would weigh 30,000 pounds; and it would take about thirty cart

loads of clay (one horse carts) to make one brick. But his account of the stones used in the building of Solomon's temple, (vol. ii. p. 211,) far exceeds his bricks of ten feet square in the walls of Babylon; these are but brick-bats compared to them. The stones (says he) employed in the foundation, were in magnitude forty cubits, (that is above sixty feet, a cubit, says he, being somewhat more than one foot and a half, (a cubit is one foot nine inches,) and the superstructure (says this Bishop) was worthy of such foundations. There were some stones, says he, of the whitest marble forty-five cubits long, five cubits high, and six cubits broad. These are the dimensions this Bishop has given, which, in measure of twelve inches to a foot, is 78 feet 9 inches long, 10 feet 6 inches broad, and 8 feet 3 inches thick, and contains 7,234 cubic feet.

I now go to demonstrate the imposition of this Bishop. A cubic foot of water weighs sixty-two pounds and a half. The specific gravity of marble to water is as 2 1-2 is to one. The weight, therefore, of a cubic foot of marble is 156 pounds, which, multiplied by 7,234, the number of cubic feet in one of those stones, makes the weight of it to be 1,128,504 pounds, which is 503 tons. Allowing then a horse to draw about half a ton, it will require a thousand horses to draw one such stone on the ground; how then were they to be lifted into the building by human hands? The Bishop may talk of faith removing mountains, but all the faith of all the Bishops that ever lived could not remove one of those stones, and their bodily strength given in.

This Bishop also tells of great guns used by the Turks at the taking of Constantinople, one of which, he says, was drawn by seventy yoke of oxen, and by two thousand men. (Vol. iii. p. 117.) The weight of a cannon that carries a ball of 43 pounds, which is the largest cannon that are cast, weighs 8,000 pounds, about three tons and a half, and may be drawn by three yoke of oxen. Any body may now calculate what the weight of the Bishop's great gun must be, that required seventy yoke of oxen to draw it. This Bishop beats Gulliver.

I pass to the last passage, in these fables of the Evangelists, called a prophecy of Jesus Christ.

John, having spoken of Jesus expiring on the cross between two thieves, says, (xix. 32, 33), "Then came the soldiers and brake the legs of the first [meaning one of the thieves] and of the other which was crucified with him. But when they came to Jesus, and saw that he was dead already, they brake not his legs." Verse 36. "For these things were done that the Scripture should be fulfilled, A bone of him shall not be broken."

The passage here referred to is in Exodus, and has no more to do with Jesus than with the ass he rode upon to Jerusalem; nor yet so much, if a roasted jack-ass, like a roasted he-goat, might be eaten at a Jewish pass-over. It might be some consolation to an ass to know that though his bones might be picked, they would not be broken. I go to state the case.

The book of Exodus, in instituting the Jewish pass-over, in which they were to eat a he-lamb, or a he-goat, says, (xii. 5), "Your lamb

---

When men give up the use of the divine gift of reason in writing on any subject, be it religious or any thing else, there are no bounds to their extravagance, no limit to their absurdities. The three volumes which this Bishop has written on what he calls the prophecies, contain above 1,200 pages, and he says in vol. iii. p. 117, "I have studied brevity." This is as marvelous as the Bishop's great gun. -- Author.

shall be without blemish, a male of the first year; ye shall take it from the sheep or from the goats." The book, after stating some ceremonies to be used in killing and dressing it, (for it was to be roasted, not boiled,) says, (ver. 43-48), "And the Lord said unto Moses and Aaron, This is the ordinance of the pass-over: there shall no stranger eat thereof; but every man's servant that is bought for money, when thou hast circumcised him, then shall he eat thereof, A foreigner shall not eat thereof. In one house shall it be eaten; thou shalt not carry forth ought of the flesh thereof abroad out of the house; neither shall ye break a bone thereof."

We here see that the case as it stands in Exodus is a ceremony and not a prophecy, and totally unconnected with Jesus's bones, or any part of him.

John, having thus filled up the measure of apostolic fable, concludes his book with something that beats all fable; for he says at the last verse, "And there are also many other things which Jesus did, the which if they could be written every one, -- I suppose that the world itself could not contain the books that should be written."[10]

This is what in vulgar life is called a thumper; that is, not only a lie, but a lie beyond the line of possibility; besides which it is an

---

[10] This belongs to the part of John now admitted to be spurious. -- Editor.

absurdity, for if they should be written in the world, the world would contain them. -- Here ends the examination of the passages called prophecies.

CONCLUSION

I have now, reader, gone through and examined all the passages which the four books of Matthew, Mark, Luke, and John, quote from the Old Testament and call them prophecies of Jesus Christ. When I first sat down to this examination, I expected to find cause for some censure, but little did I expect to find them so utterly destitute of truth, and of all pretensions to it, as I have shown them to be.

The practice which the writers of these books employ is not more false than it is absurd. They state some trifling case of the person they call Jesus Christ, and then cut out a sentence from some passage of the Old Testament and call it a prophecy of that case. But when the words thus cut out are restored to the place they are taken from, and read with the words before and after them, they give the lie to the New Testament. A short instance or two of this will suffice for the whole.

They make Joseph to dream of an angel, who informs him that Herod is dead, and tells him to come with the child out of Egypt. They then cut out a sentence from the book of Hosea, "Out of Egypt have I called my Son," and apply it as a prophecy in that case. The words, "And called my Son out of Egypt," are in the Bible. But what of that? They are only part of a passage, and not a whole passage, and stand immediately connected with other words which show they refer to the children of Israel coming out of Egypt in the time of Pharaoh, and to the idolatry they committed afterwards.

Again, they tell us that when the soldiers came to break the legs of the crucified persons, they found Jesus was already dead, and, therefore, did not break his. They then, with some alteration of the original, cut out a sentence from Exodus, "a bone of him shall not be broken," and apply it as a prophecy of that case. The words "Neither shall ye break a bone thereof," (for they have altered the text,) are in the Bible. But what of that? They are, as in the former case, only part of a passage, and not a whole passage, and when read with the words they are immediately joined to, show it is the bones of a he-lamb or a he-goat of which the passage speaks.

These repeated forgeries and falsifications create a well- founded suspicion that all the cases spoken of concerning the person called Jesus Christ are made cases, on purpose to lug in, and that very clumsily, some broken sentences from the Old Testament, and apply them as prophecies of those cases; and that so far from his being the Son of God, he did not exist even as a man -- that he is merely an imaginary or allegorical character, as Apollo, Hercules, Jupiter, and all the deities of antiquity were. There is no history written at the time Jesus Christ is said to have lived that speaks of the existence of such a person, even as a man.

Did we find in any other book pretending to give a system of religion, the falsehoods, falsifications, contradictions, and absurdities, which are to be met with in almost every page of the Old and New Testament, all the priests of the present day, who supposed themselves capable, would triumphantly shew their skill in criticism, and cry it down as a most glaring imposition. But since the books in question belong to their own trade and profession, they, or at least many of them, seek to stifle every inquiry into them and abuse those who have the honesty and the courage to do it.

When a book, as is the case with the Old and New Testament, is ushered into the world under the title of being the WORD OF GOD, it ought to be examined with the utmost strictness, in order to know if it has a well founded claim to that title or not, and whether we are or are not imposed upon: for as no poison is so dangerous as that which poisons the physic, so no falsehood is so fatal as that which is made an article of faith.

This examination becomes more necessary, because when the New Testament was written, I might say invented, the art of printing was not known, and there were no other copies of the Old Testament than written copies. A written copy of that book would cost about as much as six hundred common printed bibles now cost. Consequently the book was in the hands of very few persons, and these chiefly of the Church. This gave an opportunity to the writers of the New Testament to make quotations from the Old Testament as they pleased, and call them prophecies, with very little danger of being detected. Besides which, the terrors and inquisitorial fury of the Church, like what they tell us of the flaming sword that turned every way, stood sentry over the New Testament; and time, which brings every thing else to light, has served to thicken the darkness that guards it from detection.

Were the New Testament now to appear for the first time, every priest of the present day would examine it line by line, and compare the detached sentences it calls prophecies with the whole passages in the Old Testament from whence they are taken. Why then do they not make the same examination at this time, as they would make had the New Testament never appeared before? If it be proper and right to make it in one case, it is equally proper and right to do it in the other case. Length of time can make no difference in the right to do it at any time. But, instead of doing this, they go on as their predecessors went on before them, to tell the people there are prophecies of Jesus Christ, when the truth is there are none.

They tell us that Jesus rose from the dead, and ascended into heaven. It is very easy to say so; a great lie is as easily told as a little one. But if he had done so, those would have been the only circumstances respecting him that would have differed from the common lot of man; and, consequently, the only case that would apply exclusively to him, as prophecy, would be some passage in the Old Testament that foretold such things of him. But there is not a passage in the Old Testament that speaks of a person who, after being crucified, dead, and buried, should rise from the dead, and ascend into heaven. Our prophecy-mangers supply the silence the Old Testament guards upon such things, by telling us of passages they call prophecies, and that falsely so, about Joseph's dream, old clothes, broken bones, and such like trifling stuff.

In writing upon this, as upon every other subject, I speak a language full and intelligible. I deal not in hints and intimations. I have several reasons for this: First, that I may be clearly understood. Secondly, that it may be seen I am in earnest; and thirdly, because it is an affront to truth to treat falsehood with complaisance.

I will close this treatise with a subject I have already touched upon in the First Part of the Age of Reason.

The world has been amused with the term revealed religion, and the generality of priests apply this term to the books called the

Old and New Testament. The Mahometans apply the same term to the Koran. There is no man that believes in revealed religion stronger than I do but it is not the reveries of the Old and New Testament, nor of the Koran, that I dignify with that sacred title. That which is revelation to me, exists in something which no human mind can invent, no human hand can counterfeit or alter.

The Word of God is the Creation we behold; and this word of God revealeth to man all that is necessary for man to know of his creator. Do we want to contemplate his power? We see it in the immensity of his creation. Do we want to contemplate his wisdom? We see it in the unchangeable order by which the incomprehensible whole is governed. Do we want to contemplate his munificence? We see it in the abundance with which he fills the earth. Do we want to contemplate his mercy? We see it in his not withholding that abundance, even from the unthankful. Do we want to contemplate his will, so far as it respects man? The goodness he shows to all is a lesson for our conduct to each other.

In fine -- Do we want to know what God is? Search not the book called the Scripture, which any human hand might make, or any impostor invent; but the SCRIPTURE CALLED THE CREATION.

When, in the first part of the Age of Reason, I called the Creation the true revelation of God to man, I did not know that any other person had expressed the same idea. But I lately met with the writings of Doctor Conyers Middleton, published the beginning of last century, in which he expresses himself in the same manner, with respect to the Creation, as I have done in the Age of Reason. He was principal librarian of the University of Cambridge, in England, which furnished him with extensive opportunities of reading, and necessarily required he should be well acquainted with the dead as well as the living languages. He was a man of a strong original mind, had the courage to think for himself, and the honesty to speak his thoughts. He made a journey to Rome, from whence he wrote letters to show that the forms and ceremonies of the Romish Christian Church were taken from the degenerate state of the heathen mythology, as it stood in the latter times of the Greeks and Romans. He attacked without ceremony the miracles which the Church pretended to perform; and in one of his treatises, he calls the creation a revelation. The priests of England, of that day, in order to defend their citadel, by first defending its out- works, attacked him for attacking the Roman ceremonies; and one of them censures him for calling the creation a revelation. He thus replies to him:

"One of them," says he, "appears to be scandalized by the title of revelation which I have given to that discovery which God made of himself in the visible works of his creation. Yet it is no other than what the wise in all ages have given to it, who consider it as the most authentic and indisputable revelation which God has ever given of himself, from the beginning of the world to this day. It was this by which the first notice of him was revealed to the inhabitants of the earth, and by which alone it has been kept up ever since among the several nations of it. From this the reason of man was enabled to trace out his nature and attributes, and, by a gradual deduction of consequences, to learn his own nature also, with all the duties belonging to it, which relate either to God or to his fellow-creatures. This constitution of things was ordained by God, as an universal law, or rule of conduct to man; the source of all his knowledge; the test of all truth, by which all subsequent revelations, which are supposed to have been given by God in any other manner must be tried, and cannot be received as divine any further than as they are found to tally and coincide with this original standard.

"It was this divine law which I referred to in the passage above recited, [meaning the passage on which they had attacked him,] being desirous to excite the reader's attention to it, as it would enable him to judge more freely of the argument I was handling. For by contemplating this law, he would discover the genuine way which God himself has marked out to us for the acquisition of true knowledge; not from the authority or reports of our fellow-creatures, but from the information of the facts and material objects which, in his providential distribution of worldly things, he hath presented to the perpetual observation of our senses. For as it was from these that his existence and nature, the most important articles of all knowledge, were first discovered to man, so that grand discovery furnished new light towards tracing out the rest, and made all the inferior subjects of human knowledge more easily discoverable to us by the same method.

"I had another view likewise in the same passage, and applicable to the same end, of giving the reader a more enlarged notion of the question in dispute, who, by turning his thoughts to reflect on the works of the Creator, as they are manifested to us in this fabric of the world, could not fail to observe that they are all of them great, noble, and suitable to the majesty of his nature; carrying with them the proofs of their origin, and showing themselves to be the production of an all-wise and almighty being; and by accustoming his mind to these sublime reflections, he will be prepared to determine whether those miraculous interpositions, so confidently affirmed to us by the primitive fathers, can reasonably be thought to make a part in the grand scheme of the Divine administration, or whether it be agreeable that God, who created all things by his will, and can give what turn to them he pleases by the same will, should, for the particular purposes of his government and the services of the church, descend to the expedient of visions and revelations, granted sometimes to boys for the instruction of the elders, and sometimes to women to settle the fashion and length of their veils, and sometimes to Pastors of the Church to enjoin them to ordain one man a lecturer, another a priest; or that he should scatter a profusion of miracles around the stake of a martyr, yet all of them vain and insignificant, and without any sensible effect, either of preserving the life or easing the sufferings of the saint, or even of mortifying his persecutors, who were always left to enjoy the full triumph of their cruelty, and the poor martyr to expire in a miserable death. When these things, I say, are brought to the original test, and compared with the genuine and indisputable works of the Creator, how minute, how trifling, how contemptible must they be? And how incredible must it be thought that, for the instruction of his Church, God should employ ministers so precarious, unsatisfactory, and inadequate, as the extacies of women and boys, and the visions of interested priests, which were derided at the very time by men of sense to whom they were proposed.

"That this universal law [continues Middleton, meaning the law revealed in the works of the creation] was actually revealed to the heathen world long before the gospel was known, we learn from all the principal sages of antiquity, who made it the capital subject of their studies and writings.

"Cicero [says Middleton] has given us a short abstract of it, in a fragment still remaining from one of his books on government, which [says Middleton] I shall here transcribe in his own words, as they will illustrate my sense also, in the passages that appear so dark and dangerous to my antagonist:

"The true law, [it is Cicero who speaks] is right reason, conformable to the nature of things, constant, eternal, diffused through all, which calls us to duty by commanding, deters us from sin by forbidding; which never loses its influence with the good, nor ever preserves it with the wicked. This law cannot be over-ruled by any other, nor abrogated in whole or in part; nor can we be absolved from it either by the senate or by the people; nor are we to seek any other comment or interpreter of it but himself; nor can there be one law at Rome and another at Athens; one now and another hereafter; but the same eternal immutable law comprehends all nations at all times, under one common master and governor of all -- GOD. He is the inventor, propounder, enactor of this law; and whoever will not obey it must first renounce himself, and throw off the nature of man; by doing which, he will suffer the greatest punishments though he should escape all the other torments which are commonly believed to be prepared for the wicked.' Here ends the quotation from Cicero.

Our Doctors [continues Middleton] perhaps will look on this as RANK DEISM; but let them call it what they will, I shall ever avow and defend it as the fundamental, essential, and vital part of all true religion." Here ends the quotation from Middleton.

I have here given the reader two sublime extracts from men who lived in ages of time far remote from each other, but who thought alike. Cicero lived before the time in which they tell us Christ was born. Middleton may be called a man of our own time, as he lived within the same century with ourselves.

In Cicero we see that vast superiority of mind, that sublimity of right reasoning and justness of ideas, which man acquires, not by studying bibles and testaments, and the theology of schools built thereon, but by studying the creator in the immensity and unchangeable order of his creation, and the immutability of his law. "There cannot," says Cicero, "be one law now, and another hereafter; but the same eternal immutable law comprehends all nations, at all times, under one common master and governor of all -- GOD." But according to the doctrine of schools which priests have set up, we see one law, called the Old Testament, given in one age of the world, and another law, called the New Testament, given in another age of the world. As all this is contradictory to the eternal immutable nature, and the unerring and unchangeable wisdom of God, we must be compelled to hold this doctrine to be false, and the old and the new law, called the Old and the New Testament, to be impositions, fables, and forgeries.

In Middleton, we see the manly eloquence of an enlarged mind and the genuine sentiments of a true believer in his Creator.

Instead of reposing his faith on books, by whatever name they may be called, whether Old Testament or New, he fixes the creation as the great original standard by which every other thing called the word or work of God is to be tried. In this we have an indisputable scale where-by to measure every word or work imputed to him. If the thing so imputed carries not in itself the evidence of the same Almightiness of power, of the same unerring truth and wisdom, and the same unchangeable order in all its parts, as are visibly demonstrated to our senses, and comprehensible by our reason, in the magnificent fabric of the universe, that word or that work is not of God. Let then the two books called the Old and New Testament be tried by this rule, and the result will be that the authors of them, whoever they were, will be convicted of forgery.

The invariable principles, and unchangeable order, which regulate the movements of all the parts that compose the universe, demonstrate both to our senses and our reason that its creator is a God of unerring truth. But the Old Testament, beside the numberless absurd and bagatelle stories it tells of God, represents him as a God of deceit, a God not to be confided in. Ezekiel makes God to say, (xiv. 9), "And if the prophet be deceived when he hath spoken a thing, I, the Lord have deceived that prophet." And at xx. 25, he makes God, in speaking of the children of Israel, to say "Wherefore I gave them statutes that were not good, and judgments by which they should not live." This, so far from being the word of God, is horrid blasphemy against him. Reader, put thy confidence in thy God, and put no trust in the bible.

The same Old Testament, after telling us that God created the heavens and the earth in six days, makes the same almighty power and eternal wisdom employ itself in giving directions how a priest's garments should be cut, and what sort of stuff they should be made of, and what their offerings should be, Gold, and Silver, and Brass, and blue, and purple, and scarlet, and fine linen, and goats' hair, and rams' skins dyed red, and badger skins, etc. (xxv. 3); and in one of the pretended prophecies I have just examined, God is made to give directions how they should kill, cook, and eat a he-lamb or a he-goat. And Ezekiel, (iv.,) to fill up the measure of abominable absurdity, makes God to order him to take wheat, and barley, and beans, and lintels, and millet, and fitches, and make a loaf or a cake thereof, and bake it with human dung and eat it; but as Ezekiel complained that this mess was too strong for his stomach, the matter was compromised from man's dung to cow-dung. Compare all this ribaldry, blasphemously called the word of God, with the Almighty power that created the universe, and whose eternal wisdom directs and governs all its mighty movements, and we shall be at a loss to find a name sufficiently contemptible for it.

In the promises which the Old Testament pretends that God made to his people, the same derogatory ideas of him prevail. It makes God to promise to Abraham that his seed should be like the stars in heaven and the sand on the sea shore for multitude, and that he would give them the land of Canaan as their inheritance forever. But observe, reader, how the performance of this promise was to begin, and then ask thine own reason, if the wisdom of God, whose power is equal to his will, could, consistently with that power and that wisdom, make such a promise. The performance of the promise was to begin, according to that book, by four hundred years of bondage and affliction. Genesis xv. 13, "And he said unto Abraham, Know of a surety that thy seed shall be a stranger in a land that is not theirs, and shall serve them; and they shall afflict them four hundred years." This promise then to Abraham and his seed forever, to inherit the land of Canaan, had it been a fact instead of a fable, was to operate, in the commencement of it, as a curse upon all the people and their children, and their children's children, for four hundred years.

But the case is, the book of Genesis was written after the bondage in Egypt had taken place; and in order to get rid of the disgrace of the Lord's chosen people, as they called themselves, being in bondage to the Gentiles, they make God to be the author of it, and annex it as a condition to a pretended promise; as if God, in making that promise, had exceeded his power in performing it, and consequently his wisdom in making it, and was obliged to compromise with them for one half, and with the Egyptians, to whom they were to be in bondage, for the other half.

Without degrading my own reason by bringing those wretched and contemptible tales into a comparative view with the Almighty power and eternal wisdom, which the Creator hath demonstrated to our senses in the creation of the universe, I will confine myself to say, that if we compare them with the divine and forcible sentiments of Cicero, the result will be that the human mind has degenerated by believing them. Man, in a state of grovelling superstition from which he has not courage to rise, loses the energy of his mental powers.

I will not tire the reader with more observations on the Old Testament.

As to the New Testament, if it be brought and tried by that standard which, as Middleton wisely says, God has revealed to our senses, of his Almighty power and wisdom in the creation and government of the visible universe, it will be found equally as false, paltry, and absurd, as the Old.

Without entering, in this place, into any other argument, that the story of Christ is of human invention and not of divine origin, I will confine myself to shew that it is derogatory to God, by the contrivance of it; because the means it supposes God to use, are not adequate to the end to be obtained; and, therefore, are derogatory to the Almightiness of his power, and the eternity of his wisdom.

The New Testament supposes that God sent his Son upon earth to make a new covenant with man, which the Church calls the covenant of grace; and to instruct mankind in a new doctrine, which it calls Faith, meaning thereby, not faith in God, for Cicero and all true Deists always had and always will have this, but faith in the person called Jesus Christ; and that whoever had not this faith should, to use the words of the New Testament, be DAMNED.

Now, if this were a fact, it is consistent with that attribute of God called his goodness, that no time should be lost in letting poor unfortunate man know it; and as that goodness was united to Almighty power, and that power to Almighty wisdom, all the means existed in the hand of the Creator to make it known immediately over the whole earth, in a manner suitable to the Almightiness of his divine nature, and with evidence that would not leave man in doubt; for it is always incumbent upon us, in all cases, to believe that the Almighty always acts, not by imperfect means as imperfect man acts, but consistently with his Almightiness. It is this only that can become the infallible criterion by which we can possibly distinguish the works of God from the works of man.

Observe now, reader, how the comparison between this supposed mission of Christ, on the belief or disbelief of which they say man was to be saved or damned -- observe, I say, how the comparison between this, and the Almighty power and wisdom of God demonstrated to our senses in the visible creation, goes on.

The Old Testament tells us that God created the heavens and the earth, and everything therein, in six days. The term 'six days' is ridiculous enough when applied to God; but leaving out that absurdity, it contains the idea of Almighty power acting unitedly with Almighty wisdom, to produce an immense work, that of the creation of the universe and every thing therein, in a short time. Now as the eternal salvation of man is of much greater importance than his creation, and as that salvation depends, as the New Testament tells us, on man's knowledge of and belief in the person called Jesus Christ, it necessarily follows from our belief in the goodness and justice of God, and our knowledge of his Almighty power and wisdom, as demonstrated in the Creation, that ALL THIS, if true, would be made known to all parts of the world, in as little time at least, as was employed in making the world. To suppose the Almighty would pay greater regard and attention to the creation and organization of inanimate matter, than he would to the salvation of innumerable millions of souls, which himself had created, "as the image of himself," is to offer an insult to his goodness and his justice.

Now observe, reader, how the promulgation of this pretended salvation by a knowledge of, and a belief in Jesus Christ went on, compared with the work of creation. In the first place, it took longer time to make the child than to make the world, for nine months were passed away and totally lost in a state of pregnancy; which is more than forty times longer time than God employed in making the world, according to the bible account. Secondly, several years of Christ's life were lost in a state of human infancy. But the universe was in maturity the moment it existed. Thirdly, Christ, as Luke asserts, was thirty years old before be began to preach what they call his mission. Millions of souls died in the mean time without knowing it. Fourthly, it was above three hundred years from that time before the book called the New Testament was compiled into a written copy, before which time there was no such book. Fifthly, it was above a thousand years after that before it could be circulated; because neither Jesus nor his apostles had knowledge of, or were inspired with, the art of printing: and, consequently, as the means for making it universally known did not exist, the means were not equal to the end, and therefore it is not the work of God.

I will here subjoin the nineteenth Psalm, which is truly deistical, to shew how universally and instantaneously the works of God make themselves known, compared with this pretended salvation by Jesus Christ:

"The heavens declare the glory of God, and the firmament showeth his handiwork. Day unto day uttereth speech, and night unto night showeth knowledge. There is no speech nor language where their voice is not heard. Their line is gone out through all the earth, and their words to the end of the world. In them hath he set a chamber for the sun, which is as a bridegroom coming out of his chamber, and rejoiceth as a strong man to run a race. His going forth is from the end of the heaven, and his circuit unto the ends of it, and there is nothing hid from the heat thereof."

Now, had the news of salvation by Jesus Christ been inscribed on the face of the Sun and the Moon, in characters that all nations would have understood, the whole earth had known it in twenty-four hours, and all nations would have believed it; whereas, though it is now almost two thousand years since, as they tell us, Christ came upon earth, not a twentieth part of the people of the earth know anything of it, and among those who do, the wiser part do not believe it.

I have now, reader, gone through all the passages called prophecies of Jesus Christ, and shown there is no such thing.

I have examined the story told of Jesus Christ, and compared the several circumstances of it with that revelation which, as Middleton wisely says, God has made to us of his Power and Wisdom in the structure of the universe, and by which every thing ascribed to him is to be tried. The result is, that the story of Christ has not one trait, either in its character or in the means employed, that bears the least resemblance to the power and wisdom of God, as demonstrated in the creation of the universe. All the means are human means, slow, uncertain, and inadequate to the accomplishment of the end proposed; and therefore the whole is a fabulous invention, and undeserving of credit.

The priests of the present day profess to believe it. They gain their living by it, and they exclaim against something they call infidelity. I will define what it is. HE THAT BELIEVES IN THE STORY OF CHRIST IS AN INFIDEL TO GOD.

AUTHOR'S APPENDIX

Contradictory Doctrines Between Matthew And Mark

In the New Testament (Mark xvi. 16), it is said "He that believeth and is baptized shall be saved, but he that believeth not shall be damned."[11] This is making salvation, or, in other words, the happiness of man after this life, to depend entirely on believing, or on what Christians call faith.

But The Gospel according to Matthew makes Jesus Christ preach a direct contrary doctrine to 'The Gospel according to Mark;' for it makes salvation, or the future happiness of man, to depend entirely on 'good works;' and those good works are not works done to God, for he needs them not, but good works done to man. The passage referred to in Matthew is the account there given of what is called the last day, or the day of judgment, where the whole world is represented to be divided into two parts, the righteous and the unrighteous, metaphorically called the sheep and the goats. To the one part called the righteous, or the sheep, it says, "Come, ye blessed of my father, inherit the kingdom

---

[11] One of the concluding twelve verses not found in the earlier manuscripts of the second gospel. -- Editor.

prepared for you from the beginning of the world: for I was an hungered, and ye gave me meat: I was thirsty, and ye gave me drink: I was a stranger, and ye took me in: naked, and ye clothed me: I was sick, and ye visited me: I was in prison, and ye came unto me. Then shall the righteous answer him, saying, Lord, when saw we thee an hungered, and fed thee? or thirsty, and gave thee drink? When saw we thee a stranger, and took thee in? or naked, and clothed thee? Or when saw we thee sick, or in prison, and came unto thee? And the king shall answer and say unto them, Verily I say unto, Inasmuch as ye have done it unto one of the least of these my brethren, ye have done it unto me."

Here is nothing about believing in Christ -- nothing about that phantom of the imagination called Faith. The works here spoken of are works of humanity and benevolence, or, in other words, an endeavor to make God's creation happy. Here is nothing about preaching and making long prayers, as if God must be dictated to by man; nor about building churches and meetings, nor hiring priests to pray and preach in them. Here is nothing about predestination, that lust which some men have for damning one another. Here is nothing about baptism, whether by sprinkling or plunging, nor about any of those ceremonies for which the Christian Church has been fighting, persecuting, and burning each other ever since the Christian Church began.

If it be asked, why do not priests preach the doctrine contained in this chapter, the answer is easy: they are not fond of practicing it themselves. It does not answer for their trade. They had rather get than give. Charity with them begins and ends at home.

Had it been said, 'Come ye blessed, ye have been liberal in paying the preachers of the word, ye have contributed largely towards building churches and meeting-houses, there is not a hired priest in Christendom but would have thundered it Continually in the ears of his congregation. But as it is altogether on good works done to men, the priests pass over it in silence, and they will abuse me for bringing it into notice.

My Private Thoughts On A Future State

I have said, in the first. part of the Age of Reason, that "I hope for happiness after this life." This hope is comfortable to me, and I presume not to go beyond the comfortable idea of hope, with respect to a future state.

I consider myself in the hands of my creator, and that he will dispose of me after this life consistently with his justice and goodness. I leave all these matters to him, as my creator and friend, and I hold it to be presumption in man to make an article of faith as to what the creator will do with us hereafter.

I do not believe because a man and a woman make a child, that it imposes on the creator the unavoidable obligation of keeping the being so made in eternal existence hereafter. It is in his power to do so, or not to do so, and it is not in our power to decide which he will do.

The book called the New Testament, which I hold to be fabulous and have shown to be false, gives an account in Matthew xxv. of what is there called the last day, or the day of judgment. The whole world, according to that account, is divided into two parts, the righteous and the unrighteous, figuratively called the sheep and the goats. They are then to receive their sentence. To the one, figuratively called the sheep, it says, "Come ye blessed of my Father, inherit the kingdom prepared for you from the foundation of the world." To the other, figuratively called the goats, it says, "Depart from me, ye cursed, into everlasting fire, prepared for the devil and his angels."

Now the case is, the world cannot be thus divided: the moral world, like the physical world, is composed of numerous degrees of character, running imperceptibly one into the other, in such a manner that no fixed point of division can be found in either. That point is no where, or is everywhere. The whole world might be divided into two parts numerically, but not as to moral character; and therefore the metaphor of dividing them, as sheep and goats can be divided, whose difference is marked by their external figure, is absurd. All sheep are still sheep; all goats are still goats; it is their physical nature to be so. But one part of the world are not all good alike, nor the other part all wicked alike. There are some exceedingly good; others exceedingly wicked. There is another description of men who cannot be ranked with either the one or the other -- they belong neither to the sheep nor the goats; and there is still another description of them who are so very insignificant, both in character and conduct, as not to be worth the trouble of damning or saving, or of raising from the dead.

My own opinion is, that those whose lives have been spent in doing good, and endeavoring to make their fellow-mortals happy, for this is the only way in which we can serve God, will be happy hereafter and that the very wicked will meet with some punishment. But those who are neither good nor bad, or are too insignificant for notice, will be drooped entirely. This is my opinion. It is consistent with my idea of God's justice, and with the reason that God has given me, and I gratefully know that he has given me a large share of that divine gift.

DO YOU LIKE MYSTERIES OF HUMANKIND SUCH AS PROPHECIES OR LEGENDS?

Then take a look
at the following books

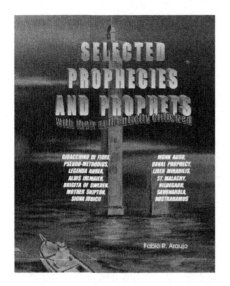

One night, an Italian painter had a nightmare... He saw his city flooded looking from a certain room on the last floor of his house. The flood was huge, it couldn't be just a rain. Later he knew that at the same night, one of his sisters had exactly the same dream... and her dream had the same details of his dream... then he painted what he saw. He lives in Bologna, a city famous for its two towers. You can see them here and maybe the painting shows our post-global-warming time.

ONLY US$ 14.99

I n *Selected Prophecies and Prophets, you will see*

- How Nostradamus foresaw Putin as the Antichrist

- What might be the oldest prophecy in the world with the word "America." This prophecy has never been published before anywhere, and the author found it in a manuscript in a European library; it is translated from the Latin manuscript into English for the first time. The prophecy says the "Muslims will arrive in America." Could that be about the 9/11 2001?

- The Adso manuscript as presented by Sackur, translated from Latin into English

- Many old prophecies translated from the original text from different languages (Old Italian, Old French, German, etc.) into English, from the book which first published the prophecy, including the Leonardo da Vinci prophecies, which are in manuscripts in Paris, the Orval Prophecy, the 16th century Liber Mirabilis, Alois Irlmaier prophecies, etc. The writer went directly to the sources.

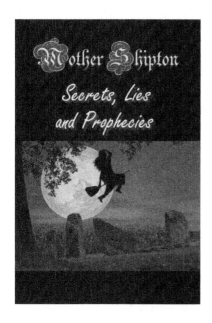

Secrets, lies, and prophecies. That will be one's experience if the subject is Mother Shipton. But who is Mother Shipton? Some will consider her the most famous prophet in the last 1000 years, after Nostradamus. In fact, she might be the most famous prophetess in the world's history. If some think she really existed and was a soothsayer or maybe an astrologer who predicted facts (most of them regarding the 17th century or about our own future), others may believe that she is no more than a legend slowly built over the years.

US$ 9.99

*7*n *Mother Shipton, you will see*

- The facts and legends about her

- Who was she and what were her REAL prophecies

- The prophecies attributed to her through the history

- The last prophecy attributed to her in the 20th century

- The Kirby Cemetery mystery explained

Peter Lemesurier, world-wide famous writer, author of *The Unknown Nostradamus* and *Nostradamus: The Illustrated Prophecies* said:

"This book offers a broad survey of what is known about mother Shipton and her supposed prophecies, and wisely comes to no very firm conclusions."

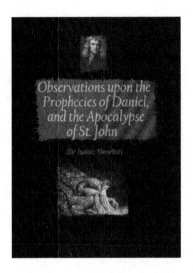

Maybe you know that Isaac Newton went to the University to prove God exists, but do you know about his interest on prophecies and his interpretation on the Apocalypse of St. John and the prophecies of Daniel? In fact, Newton devoted most of his life to study of the Scripture and prophecies in general. He naturally believed in the end of the world.

US$ 9.50

In this book, you will see

- The local conditions when the Apocalypse was written

- The conditions he believed were related to the second coming of Christ

- Some important statements about the history of the Church

The same author of Selected Prophecies and Prophets, who is a Historian who has been researching prophecies the matter for 20 years. In this book, he presents many legends and myths about a past pole shift, a past global warming and a past huge flood, from different civilizations and compares them to prophecies about the global warming a and a future flood.

US$ 14.50

In Global Warming, Global Flood, you will see

- Many impressive myths and legends about a past pole shift and a past flood (which happened when the ice melted after the shift), which changed the position the sun sets.

- Prophecies about the 3 days of darkness, which are linked to this global catastrophe, according to the author.

- Evidences to show that a global warming is not happening, but part of the South Hemisphere is getting colder, while the North Hemisphere is getting hotter.

- An amazing prophecy about the global warming printed in the 1950s, which says

"The scientists will believe in many theories to explain the changes in the weather, such as global warming, but will not accept the idea of a slow pole shift, which comes before the big catastrophe".

" This world will last six thousand years: two thousand years without law, two thousand years under the Torah and two thousand years will be the days of the Messiah." [12]

---

[12] This 3 thousand year old prophecy is attributed to Tanna debe Eliyyahu. The 2 thousand years without law are the years from the biblical creation to Abraham. According to Historians and the tradition, Abraham left the Sumerian Ur about 2000 BC. Since then until Christ, more 2 thousand years passed, which are the years under the Torah. From Christ the Messiah to our time, more 2 thousand years were counted. This prophecy is clear: We are near the end of the world.

In the book Global Warming, Global Flood, you will find the following found in some versions of the Corpus Hermeticum, which was not included in some versions. The author, Historian, says the following:

I found this prophecy in a printed version of the *Corpus Hermeticum*, but I've seen versions without it. The *Corpus Hermeticum* is an old book and very well-known all over the world, mainly for people with some esoteric or occult knowledge. It seems that the *Corpus Hermeticum's* text was written between 2nd century BC and 3rd century AD. The text consists of a set of writings that arrived to us in Greek. The Latin translation of the text, done by Marsilio Ficino, was as incunable[13], printed for the first time in 1471. Later it was translated into other languages. And later, in other editions, the *Corpus Hermeticum* received additions. This work was attributed to mythical Hermes Trismegistus (meaning "Hermes three times big"). This text had a certain importance in the first centuries of the Church and it was popular until the Middle Ages, having inspired hermetic writings which started to bloom at that time. In the end of the 17th century, some writers stated that this text was a fake. This hypothesis had to be totally denied when *Corpus Hermeticum* manuscripts were found in 1945 in *Nag Hammadi*, Egypt, in Coptic, which was the last phase of the Egyptian language, and was spoken by the Christians in Egypt in the first centuries.[14] This very old text has some interesting prophecies, located in the final part of the work. It predicts a flood, which will be a divine instrument for a recreation:

"The earth will lose its balance then, the sea will stop being navigable, the sky won't be full of stars, the stars will stop their

---

[13] Printed before 1500.
[14] According to Athanasius Kircher (1602-1680), an important German Jesuit scholar, Hermes Trismegistus was Moses.

march through the sky, all divine voice will be forced to silence and they will remain silent, the fruits of the earth will rot, the soil will stop being fertile, the air will get ill in a dismal torpor. This will happen because of the old age of the world: irreligion, disorder, and irrational confusion in everything. When these things happen, oh Asclepius, then the Lord and the Father, the God first in power... will annihilate all the malice, destroying it through a flood, consuming it through the fire, killing it through pestilential illnesses extended to several places, but soon it will drive the world to its beauty as it was in the beginning, so that this same world becomes again worthy of reverence and admiration and so that also God, creator and restorer of such a big work, be glorified by men so that they live, then, with continuous praise, hymns and blessings. In reality, in this moment it will be the birth of the world: a renewal for the good things, a sacred and solemn restoration of the nature, imposed by force as time goes by (...) One day will come when the man will prefer to produce the food with their hands, but the food will be poison. Man will poison the earth, the water and the sky and it will end up also poisoning his heart... A scythe will harvest the victims and a hammer will knead the men."

Printed in Great Britain
by Amazon

46830763R00066